THE VICTORIANS

Usborne Quicklinks

The Usborne Quicklinks Website is packed with thousands of links to all the best websites on the internet. The websites include information, video clips, sounds, games and animations that support and enhance the information in Usborne internet-linked books.

To visit the recommended websites for this book, go to the Usborne Quicklinks Website at **www.usborne.com/quicklinks** and enter the keywords **The Victorians**.

When using the internet please follow the internet safety guidelines displayed on the Usborne Quicklinks Website. The recommended websites in Usborne Quicklinks are regularly reviewed and updated, but Usborne Publishing Ltd. is not responsible for the content or availability of any website other than its own. We recommend that children are supervised while using the internet.

V THE ICTORIANS

Ruth Brocklehurst

Illustrated by Ian McNee

Designed by Brenda Cole & Stephen Moncrieff

Edited by Jane Chisholm

Consultant: Dr. Hilary Fraser,
Birkbeck College, University of London

Contents

Nineteenth century Britain

In 1837, King William IV died, and his young niece Victoria was crowned Queen of Great Britain and Ireland. She was only 18 years old, but she would become Britain's longest reigning monarch so far.

During her 64 year rule, the Victorians built up a vast empire overseas, and achieved enormous social, economic and scientific progress at home. By the time Queen Victoria died, in 1901, Britain had become the wealthiest, most powerful nation in the world.

The young queen

At four, Victoria, like all children of the time, was dressed as a miniature adult.

People often picture Queen Victoria as she was in the last years of her reign – a grumpy, disapproving old lady. But this was far from true of the teenage girl who came to the throne. Although Victoria always took her royal duties very seriously, her diaries show that she was passionate and fun-loving too. As a girl, she enjoyed dressing in bright silks for the opera and attending lavish balls at Buckingham Palace.

Victoria was born in Kensington Palace, in London, in 1819 and christened Alexandrina Victoria. Her uncle, William IV, and his wife had no surviving children, so it soon became clear that Victoria would succeed him to the throne.

The young heiress had a strict, lonely upbringing, with little company apart from her over-protective mother and her governess. Despite her solitude, Victoria was a lively, playful child who enjoyed painting, riding, music, singing and dancing.

Learning to be a queen

Walking tall

Victoria was taught to walk in a regal manner by balancing books on her head and having prickly holly leaves tied under her chin.

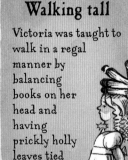

As well as the usual school subjects, such as languages and mathematics, Princess Victoria felt it was her duty to study the kings and queens of Britain, in preparation for her future role. "A great queen but a bad woman," was how she described one of her predecessors, Queen Elizabeth I.

The princess also had to learn how to walk, talk and act like royalty. She was made to keep a special book, where she noted everything she did and how she behaved, especially when she was naughty. Entries that she made in this book, and in her personal diaries, showed that although she was anxious to be good, Victoria was often stubborn and quick-tempered too.

Public image

When Victoria became queen in 1837, public opinion of the monarchy was at an all time low. Her predecessors had been unpopular – George IV was seen as wasteful and sleazy and William IV was old and doddery. Their reigns had seen public protests and bloody riots, and some people even thought Britain might be on the brink of a revolution. Victoria was determined to restore the image of the monarchy. So it was vital that she made a good impression at her first major public event – her coronation.

It was a splendid, dignified affair. During the ceremony, an elderly lord tripped near the throne and Victoria helped him to his feet. This kind gesture won the people's hearts and convinced them that their new queen would be caring, humble and respectable. To them, she became known as England's rose.

This painting of the young Queen Victoria is by Franz Xavier Winterhalter, a German artist who painted more than 120 portraits of Victoria and her family.

Queen Victoria's family tree

GEORGE III
(1760-1820)

| Frederick, Duke of York | Charlotte, Princess Royal | 10 others |

| GEORGE IV (1820-1830) | WILLIAM IV (1830-1837) | Edward, Duke of Kent |

Charlotte
(died in childbirth, with no surviving children)

VICTORIA
(1837-1901)

The dates show the years of each monarch's reign.

7

Victoria and Albert

One of Victoria's main duties as Queen was to marry and produce an heir. Her German cousin Albert, Duke of Saxe-Coburg-Gotha, had been regarded by her family as a suitable match for her from early on. When they first met at 17, they didn't get along. Victoria could be hot-headed and rash, while Albert was cool and rational. But their differences brought out the best in each other and they grew to be a devoted couple.

Two years later, on October 15, 1839, Victoria asked Albert to marry her – it would have been improper for a prince to propose to the Queen – and he accepted. The following year, on February 10, hordes of cheering Londoners crowded outside Buckingham Palace to catch a glimpse of their Queen as her coach drove past. Victoria's dress was made of white satin and lace. In her hair were diamonds and orange blossoms. Over her heart she wore a diamond and sapphire brooch – a gift from Albert.

Prince Albert cuts a dashing figure in fashionable formal dress, including a top hat and tail coat.

Married life

Prince Albert was a quiet, clever man. He was happy for Victoria to take the limelight, but he was frustrated that he had no official title or duty. At first, his only job was to blot Victoria's signature on official papers. Gradually, Victoria relied more and more on his help and advice, until they were effectively ruling together. But parliament refused to make Albert King. So in 1857, Victoria gave him the title of Prince Consort, in recognition of his importance to her and the country.

The royal family

Victoria and Albert had nine children, and many Victorians saw them as the ideal happy family. For most of the year they lived in Windsor Castle, but they also had two country homes – Osborne House, on the Isle of Wight, and Balmoral Castle, in Scotland – where they could escape the formality of public life. The couple worked in the mornings and spent the rest of the day with their children, enjoying simple pastimes such as walking, riding and painting.

Victoria was anxious to see her children as happily married as she was and, when they grew up, she urged them to marry European royalty. When they began to have families of their own, she earned the nickname the Grandmama of Europe. Victoria hoped that their family ties would ensure future peace. But, sadly, when the First World War broke out in 1914, two of her grandsons, King George V and Kaiser Wilhelm II of Germany, were on opposing sides.

Victoria and Albert pose for an informal family portrait with their children.

Politics and power

By Victorian times, Britain was a constitutional monarchy. This meant that political power rested with the government, not with the Queen. But she still held some influence, so ministers had to try to get along with her.

Ten prime ministers held office during Victoria's reign, and power swung between two main parties. The Whigs – later called the Liberals – supported political reform, while the Conservatives, or Tories, were usually against change. Victoria's first prime minister was the Whig, Lord Melbourne. He spent hours with her every day, teaching her about the business of government, and soon became like a father to her.

Victorian politicians wore long coats and top hats to Parliament. Etiquette dictated that they had to remove their hats when addressing the chamber.

The Houses of Parliament were designed by Charles Barry after the original buildings were destroyed in a fire in 1834. Queen Victoria opened the new parliament buildings in 1852.

Victoria grew so attached to Melbourne that when the Tories came to power in 1841 she almost refused to accept them. Eventually, Prince Albert persuaded her to remain above party politics and to cooperate with the new prime minister, Sir Robert Peel. In time, Victoria grew to admire him.

Political change

British politics had become more democratic during the late Georgian period, but it was still very different from today. At the start of Victoria's reign, only wealthy landowners could stand for Parliament, fewer than one in seven men could vote, and women weren't allowed to take part in elections at all.

In 1838, a group of workers published a people's charter demanding electoral reforms. The government rejected the charter, and after a decade of campaigning the movement declined. But, by the end of Victoria's reign many of the Chartists' reforms had been introduced.

Chartist demands

The Chartists made six demands, which they hoped would help to improve the lives of working people, by giving them a say in how the country was run.

PEOPLE'S CHARTER

1. Votes for all men over the age of 21

2. Votes to be secret

3. Candidates to stand for election regardless of their wealth

4. A salary for members of Parliament

5. All electoral districts to be of equal size

6. Elections to take place every year

The Chartists staged public rallies and strikes. They also took petitions to the government in 1839, 1842 and 1848.

The first petition was said to contain 11 million signatures and was three miles long.

Hard times

Life in the Houses of Parliament and Buckingham Palace was full of pomp and ceremony, but for ordinary people it was a very different story. Many Victorians faced a daily struggle against poverty and hardship, and had little chance of making things better.

In the late 18th century, most British people lived a rural life, working as farmers or as craftsmen producing handmade goods. Then, new machines were invented that could do the work in a fraction of the time. This left thousands unemployed, so they flocked to the towns in search of new jobs. This radical change in the way people lived and worked became known as the Industrial Revolution.

Daily bread

The Industrial Revolution made a small number of people incredibly wealthy, but for most, the 1830s and 40s were tough. Jobs remained scarce and wages were pitifully low. To make matters worse, bread became so expensive that many couldn't afford it. This was because of a new law called the Corn Law, which prevented the importing of cheap grain. It was supposed to protect the incomes of British farmers, but it also pushed up the price of bread, especially in the years when there was a bad harvest. The situation became so dire that people were starving in the streets.

A group of politicians and industrialists got together to campaign for an end to the Corn Law, and for fairer wages. Other groups, including religious charities such as the Salvation Army and Dr. Barnardo's, took more direct action to relieve the distress of the starving. They ran soup kitchens and orphanages, and provided clothing and shelters for the needy.

A few parents couldn't afford to look after their children. Dr. Barnardo's charity took care of homeless children, like these, and gave them shelter and education.

What's cooking?

Alexis Soyer was a chef at a top London restaurant, where he cooked lavish meals for wealthy celebrities.

But he also set up soup kitchens in London and across Ireland to feed starving paupers.

Poor relief

For the very poorest people, the last resort was to go to places called workhouses. The government made sure that nobody saw the workhouse as an easy option. Once inside, families were split up, as men, women and children – and those who were too old or too sick to work – were made to live in separate quarters, which were often crowded and dirty.

Inmates had to work very long hours. Women were usually given domestic chores like cooking and cleaning, while men were given heavy work including breaking rocks and chopping wood. All this was done on a diet of potatoes, bread, cheese and soup, served in small portions that often left people still hungry. If a man left the workhouse, his family had to leave too. But if he didn't find a job, they'd soon end up back inside.

The Victorian author Charles Dickens wrote about the suffering of the poor in many of his books, which were often based on his own experiences. His family had been imprisoned for debt when he was 12.

This illustration from Dickens's novel, *Oliver Twist*, shows Oliver in the workhouse, daring to ask for more food.

Troubles in Ireland

This Victorian Irish family
was forced to live in this
hut after being evicted
from their farm for failing
to pay their rent.

Relations between Britain and Ireland had been uneasy
for centuries. But since 1801 Ireland had been part of
the United Kingdom, ruled by the British government
in London. While a few Irish people prospered under
British rule, most lived as farmers in dreadful poverty
and many held the government to blame.

Most of Ireland's farmland belonged to wealthy
landowners who employed agents to manage their
estates for them. The agents then leased the land to
local farmers. The more tenants they had, the more
rent they collected, so they divided the land into the
smallest farms possible. The poor farmers had barely
enough land to grow what they needed to survive.

In 1845, disaster struck. The Irish potato crop became infected with a fungal disease, called blight, which turned the potatoes to an inedible black pulp. Potatoes were the staple diet and many farmers had almost no other crops to fall back on. The next two years also saw failed harvests. Unable to pay their rent, thousands were evicted, left starving and homeless. To reduce the price of bread and to feed the starving, Robert Peel ended the Corn Law. But it was too little, too late. By 1850, over a million people had died.

Home Rule

After the famine, many Irish people felt that the government hadn't done enough to help. Some wanted independence from Britain, and a few were even prepared to use violence to achieve it. But an Irish politician named Charles Stuart Parnell ran a peaceful campaign for 'Home Rule' – for the Irish to have their own parliament. He called for fairer rents and for farmers to be given the chance to buy their own farms.

By 1885, Parnell's Home Rule party had 86 members of Parliament in London. They convinced Prime Minister William Gladstone that Home Rule was the best way to make peace in Ireland. He tried twice to pass an Irish Home Rule Bill, but was defeated by politicians who feared that it might encourage other parts of the British empire to claim independence. In 1890, Parnell was involved in a divorce scandal and forced out of office in disgrace. Without him, the Home Rule cause was weakened and the Irish problem remained unresolved for the rest of Victoria's reign.

Setting sail

About two million people left Ireland, mostly going to America, in search of a better life. By 1850, the Irish made up a quarter of the populations of New York city and Boston.

Irish peasants waiting for a ship to take them to America

In this cartoon, Gladstone – shown as a kangaroo – is defending Ireland against his political rival, Lord Salisbury in a boxing match.

15

Coal, steam and steel

The Industrial Revolution rapidly gained pace as engineers developed steam engines with enough power to drive whole factories. This led to a massive increase in manufacturing in Britain and enabled the Victorians to dominate world trade. By the mid-19th century, industrial output was so high that Britain became known as the workshop of the world.

Raw power

The raw materials that made the Industrial Revolution possible were coal and iron. Coal fired the steam engines, and most machines were made from iron. In 1856, Henry Bessemer invented a method for converting iron into steel cheaply and in bulk. Steel is lighter, stronger and less brittle than iron, so this meant that engineers could build bigger and better ships, bridges, buildings and machinery than ever before.

The men in this Victorian painting are stoking the huge blast furnace of a Bessemer steel converter.

This photograph from 1865 shows a group of shipyard bosses wearing 'stovepipe' hats. Behind them, a large ship is being built and smoke belches out from the chimneys of dockside steelworks and factories.

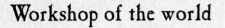

Workshop of the world

By the 1850s, more than half the world's textile goods were made in the huge mills that sprang up across the north of England and Scotland. And in the major ports, shipbuilding grew at an even greater rate. By the 1890s, over three quarters of all the ships in the world were British-built. But all this came at a price.

Workers, including thousands of young children, were often expected to work for up to 12 hours a day in unhealthy and dangerous conditions. Over time, the government introduced laws, enforcing a minimum age for child workers, limiting the number of hours people should work and setting safety standards.

Child workers

Before the government brought in laws to protect child workers, many endured tough, dangerous jobs for very little pay.

'Putters' hauled coal up from the mines along passages that were too narrow for adults to squeeze through.

In textile factories, 'scavengers' had to crawl inside working machines to pick up loose threads. Many got caught in the machinery and were badly injured.

Urban sprawl

National statistics

In 1837, only around a fifth of the British population lived in towns. By the end of Victoria's reign in 1901, the population had more than doubled to 40 million people, and three quarters of them lived in the rapidly expanding towns and cities.

As industry grew, more and more people moved to the towns and cities to find work. In 1851, the government carried out a survey, called a census, to find out exactly how many people there were in Britain, where they lived and what they did for a living. It showed that, for the first time anywhere in the world, more of the population lived in the towns than in the countryside.

This scene shows a Victorian town from around 1851.

Factory smoke pollutes the air.

Suburbs

Houses are crammed back-to-back in rows called terraces.

Up to 20 people live in each tiny house.

Houses are heated by coal fires.

Gas lamp

Chimney sweep

Water comes from a shared pump.

Life in the slums

Most people lived in filthy, crowded parts of the town, known as slums. In some slums people lived in decrepit old buildings that were barely standing. Elsewhere, the slums were made up of rows and rows of cheap new houses built hastily by factory owners for their workers to live in. These houses didn't have toilets or running water. Instead, people shared a communal lavatory, which was usually just a hole in the ground in a shed. Water came from a pump in the street, or from a nearby river.

Most household waste was tipped out into the streets or into the rivers, so they became polluted. With so many people living in these appalling conditions, it's hardly surprising that diseases spread rapidly through the slums and life expectancy was extremely low.

Trading up

Since the end of the Corn Law, the government had relaxed the laws restricting the trade of other goods too. Business boomed under this new policy of free trade, new jobs were created and life gradually got better for many people.

Among those who profited most were factory owners, bankers and businessmen. A number of modern British department stores began in the 19th century as market stalls and small shops that expanded. Soon, anyone who could afford it moved to large houses in the suburbs, away from the dirt and noise of the slums.

Street life

Poor Victorians found all kinds of ways to make money on the busy city streets.

Young boys offered shoe shines for a few pennies.

Others cleared away horse manure.

Girls sold bunches of flowers or boxes of matches on street corners.

Costermongers sold fruit and vegetables from barrows...

...those who were really successful later opened their own shops.

19

Law and order

"Send him to jail now, and you make him a jail-bird for life."

Sherlock Holmes, in *The Adventure of the Blue Carbuncle*, suggests that prison isn't always the best solution to crime.

This cartoon shows a bobby on the beat. The uniform was designed so that the police didn't look like a miltary force.

Top hat

Blue tail coat

Policeman in uniform from the 1830s

Shifty youth

As Britain's towns and cities swelled, crime levels soared at an alarming rate. Sensational accounts of crimes were regularly published in the popular press, which raised people's fears. Something had to be done to deal with the problem. The Victorian solutions were police and prisons.

On the beat

In 1829, Robert Peel established the Metropolitan police in London. The policemen were soon nicknamed 'bobbies' or 'peelers' after Robert Peel. The police force gradually grew, and by 1856 it covered the whole country.

The main task of the police was to patrol the streets, to prevent crime and protect people and their property. But their duties also included lighting street lamps and calling out the time. Anyone caught committing a crime faced harsh punishment – including imprisonment, flogging or being shipped to penal colonies in Australia.

Police kit

As well as their uniforms, Victorian bobbies were issued with various tools.

They had a whistle, to raise the alarm...

...handcuffs to restrain suspects...

...and a wooden truncheon.

Behind bars

It didn't take much to get sent to prison. Police records show that children as young as eight were jailed for crimes as petty as stealing a loaf of bread. Most Victorians believed that prisons were for punishment, rather than rehabilitation. So they designed the prison experience to be as unpleasant as possible, to deter people from committing crimes. In some prisons, inmates were blindfolded and kept silent at all times so they couldn't communicate with one another.

This detail from a painting, by Willian Powell Frith, shows convicts trudging around the exercise yard of Millbank Prison.

Dr. Watson

Sherlock Holmes

Detective work

Despite these strict new measures, a number of particularly gruesome crimes hit the headlines. One of the most infamous was that of a serial killer nicknamed Jack the Ripper, who terrorized London's East End in the 1880s. It was one of the first cases in which police collected forensic, or scientific, evidence from the crime scenes. Jack the Ripper was never caught, but forensic science later became a vital part of detective work.

Forensic science was made popular by Arthur Conan Doyle's fictional detective, Sherlock Holmes. He is shown here testing some evidence.

All aboard

The first rail passengers had to travel in dirty open wagons.

But, as rail travel took off, it became more comfortable. Plush seating, dining cars and lavatories were added to passenger trains.

Queen Victoria made frequent rail journeys in her own luxurious royal carriage.

Rain, Steam and Speed – The Great Western Railway, painted in 1839-1844 by J.M.W. Turner

Railway mania

It wasn't only the growth of towns, cities, and factories that transformed Victorian Britain. The railways also grew rapidly during this period, making an enormous impact on people's working lives, their social lives and the landscape.

Trains pulled by steam engines – known as locomotives – provided a quick, efficient way to transport raw materials and finished goods in bulk, and helped British industries to grow. Soon, they became a popular way to get around, too.

Until Victorian times, most people in Britain had never been further than the next town. The first passenger train was launched in 1825, but it wasn't until the middle of the 19th century that passenger travel really took off. As the Victorians built up a vast network of local and national train lines, the trains made it quicker, easier and cheaper to travel across the country than ever before.

Making tracks

Rail travel became popular with everyone, and the railways grew at an astonishing rate. To meet the growing demand, train companies and travel agents sprang up, offering excursions to the seaside, to exhibitions and even to public executions. Between 1845 and 1900, the number of passengers on Britain's railways tripled. By the end of the 19th century, over 29,000km (18,000 miles) of steel track had been forged and laid, criss-crossing the entire country.

It's difficult to imagine now, but people around the country used to set their watches to different times, depending on where they lived. For example, Oxford was five minutes behind London. This caused chaos with train timetables – people missed connections and there were even a few crashes when trains from rail companies using different local times tried to stop at the same platform at the same time. Gradually, rail companies all switched to London time and in 1880 it was finally adopted by the whole country, by law.

This Victorian railway poster advertises the route between England and Scotland. The map shows how the rail network extends across the country.

Great exhibitions

In 1851, the Victorians staged one of the most exciting and ambitious events of the age – the Great Exhibition. It was masterminded by Prince Albert to celebrate Britain's industry and its empire. It was an enormous show of arts, produce and manufactured goods housed in Crystal Palace, a gigantic structure of glass and steel, built specially for the event in Hyde Park, in the heart of London.

Crystal Palace was designed by Joseph Paxton, a former gardener who based the idea on a greenhouse. The building was the first of its kind, and a spectacular tribute to British engineering.

This is Joseph Paxton's first rough design for Crystal Palace. He drew it very sketchily, on blotting paper, and you can see where the ink has spattered and spread.

Queen Victoria opened the Great Exhibition on May 1, 1851. Over the next six months, millions of people from all over the country visited London to see it. Among the rare and exotic things on show were furs from Russia, an entire Turkish bazaar and a Tunisian nomads' tent covered in lion skins. But what excited people most was the machine hall. This housed an awesome display of new technology – from printing presses and threshing machines to steam engines. The Crystal Palace was like a crystal ball, offering its visitors a vision of the wider world and of the future.

Albert's legacy

The Great Exhibition ended in October 1851, having made a massive profit. Prince Albert used that money to set up the Royal Colleges of Music and Art, the Imperial College of Science and several museums. These included the Natural History Museum, the Science Museum and what is now called the Victoria and Albert Museum. Entry to the museums was free, so that everyone could enjoy them. Soon, museums and art galleries sprang up in towns all around Britain.

Show of numbers

2,700 men were employed to build the Crystal Palace in just six months.

It was made from 300,000 panes of hand-blown glass.

Crystal Palace covered an area the size of four soccer fields.

13,000 exhibits were put on display.

6,000,000 people visited the Great Exhibition.

Queen Victoria and her family visited the exhibition 13 times.

This painting shows the front entrance of Crystal Palace. Along the roof are the flags of all the nations that took part.

Natural history

The work of leading Victorian naturalists brought many new ideas about the natural world to the public. Some of these ideas sparked controversy, and revolutionized the way people thought about their place in the world.

Walking with dinosaurs

The dinosaur park at Crystal Palace in Sydenham (see below) became a fashionable place for Victorians to take a stroll.

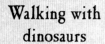

The park included 15 different species of dinosaurs and extinct creatures.

Monsters from the past

For centuries, people had been digging up mysterious giant bones, but no one knew what they were. By the 1820s, most scientists believed that they were the fossilized remains of huge, ancient reptiles. In 1842, scientist Richard Owen studied these fossils and found that they belonged to a group that was quite distinct from reptiles. He named them dinosaurs, which means 'terrible lizard' in Greek.

The model dinosaurs were made from cast iron and painted to look as lifelike as possible.

Crystal Palace burned down in 1936, but the park and the dinosaurs are still there today.

Unfortunately, experts now consider Owen's model dinosaurs to be very inaccurate.

After the Great Exhibition, the Crystal Palace was taken down and rebuilt in the London suburb of Sydenham. There, Richard Owen oversaw the creation of one of its greatest attractions: a dinosaur park, where people could wander among life-size models of prehistoric creatures in supposedly natural settings among shrubs and ponds.

A cathedral to nature

In 1856, Richard Owen became the superintendant of the British Museum's natural history collection. He wanted to arrange specimens in groups by species to show their common features. But there wasn't enough room in the British Museum. So he persuaded the government that a new building was needed. What he called his grand 'cathedral to nature' in South Kensington, in London, is now known as the Natural History Museum.

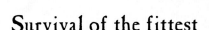

Visitors to the Natural History Museum admired all kinds of exhibits, including a model of a dodo – a bird that has been extinct since the 1660s.

Survival of the fittest

In 1859, the English scientist Charles Darwin published his radical theory of evolution, suggesting that species of plants and animals had developed, or evolved, over millions of years. This allowed them to adapt as the environment changed, so that the species that adapted best survived and passed on their characteristics to their offspring.

Most Victorians believed that God had created all living things at the same time and so many were outraged at Darwin's theory. There was even a public debate between the scientist Thomas Henry Huxley, who supported Darwin, and Samuel Wilberforce, the Bishop of Oxford, who spoke against him. The argument caused such uproar that one shocked lady in the audience fainted and had to be carried out.

Despite the controversy at the time, Darwinian theory now forms the basis of much modern thinking about the natural sciences. But, more than a century later, Darwin's ideas continue to cause debate, as some people still object to them on religious grounds.

This Victorian cartoon of Charles Darwin pokes fun at his idea that people had evolved from apes.

The Crimean War

Sites of the Crimean War

RUSSIA

Sea of
Azov

Black
Sea

CRIMEA

Alma

Inkerman

Sevastopol Balaklava

"Forward, the Light Brigade!
Charge for the guns!" he said:
Into the valley of Death
Rode the six hundred.

Lines from *The Charge
of the Light Brigade*,
by Alfred, Lord Tennyson

One of the bloodiest, most disorganized wars in European history took place in 1854-1856, in the Crimea, a region by the Black Sea between Russia and Turkey. It broke out when Russian forces attacked the Turkish fleet. The British and French governments were anxious to limit Russia's power in the area, so they joined forces with the Turks to fight against Russia.

The war became notorious for the huge numbers of soldiers who died on both sides. As many as half the 1,200,000 who went to fight lost their lives, often due to the incompetence of their officers.

The most disastrous battle took place at Balaklava, when a British cavalry unit, the Light Horse Brigade, was mistakenly ordered to charge at the enemy through a narrow valley. The Russians above the valley, simply bombarded the horsemen with cannon fire. Of 673 men in the charge, 118 were killed, 127 wounded, and over half of the men's horses died.

This is a scene from *The Charge of the Light Brigade*, a movie made in 1968, about the Battle of Balaklava.

Although many soldiers were killed in battle, thousands more died as a result of their appalling living conditions. The army camps and hospitals were crowded and insanitary, and soldiers didn't have enough food, clothing or medical supplies. Many fell prey to diseases such as cholera and malaria, while others died from infected wounds, exposure and starvation.

One thing was entirely new though: this was the first war ever to have journalists and photographers on the spot, recording events as they unfolded. Back at home, people could read the shocking horrors of the war in their daily copies of *The Times*. The news caused a public outcry and led two remarkable women to take decisive action.

Queen Victoria was so troubled by the reports of the conditions in the Crimea, that she set about knitting mittens, hats and scarves to send to her troops at the front.

Florence Nightingale became known as the 'Lady with the lamp' because she made regular night rounds of her wards.

Angels of mercy

A British nurse named Florence Nightingale took 38 nurses from England to Turkey to work in the army hospitals. Within weeks, they had cut the number of soldiers dying in hospitals from 42% to 2% – mainly by improving hygiene.

Closer to the front, a Jamaican woman named Mary Seacole often treated men on the battlefield itself. To pay for medical supplies, she set up a guest house called the British Hotel, where she sold food and drink to soldiers and took care of the sick and wounded.

The war finally ended in the spring of 1856, when the Russian Emperor, Alexander II, signed a peace treaty at the Congress of Paris. But British generals and politicians argued for years over who was to blame for the charge of the Light Brigade.

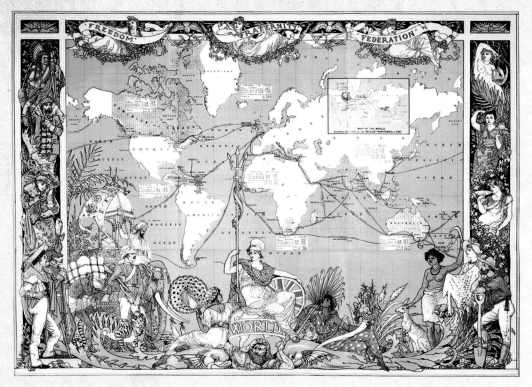

The pink areas on this Victorian world map show the extent of the British empire in 1886.

The lines across the oceans show the global trade routes. These were all under British control.

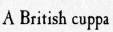

A British cuppa

Tea became a popular everyday drink in Britain in Victorian times, when it was imported in bulk from China, India and Sri Lanka.

The jewel in the crown

One of the reasons why the British got drawn into the Crimean War was to protect their trade shipping routes and their growing empire in Africa and Asia. People called it "the empire on which the sun never set" because it reached every corner of the globe. And India became one of Queen Victoria's most prized imperial possessions.

Since the 1600s, a British trading company called the East India Company had gained control of a number of Indian ports and settlements, where they set up colonies. Gradually, the Company took over more and more land and built up an army of British and local soldiers. By the start of Victoria's reign, large parts of India were technically in British hands, but not yet under British rule.

The Indian mutiny

Then, in 1856, something happened to change things dramatically. A story spread among the Indian soldiers in the East India Company's army that they had been issued with rifle cartridges smeared with cow and pig fat. This offended Hindu and Muslim soldiers, who mutinied, refusing to follow the orders of their officers. The mutiny soon led to violent clashes that spread across northern India and lasted 13 months. Thousands died, but eventually the British managed to restore their authority.

Sepoys

Indian foot soldiers in the British Army were known as sepoys. They came from all over India and included Sikhs, Muslims and Hindus.

This sepoy wears a turban with his uniform.

Empress Victoria

A year later, the British government decided that the only solution was to take direct control. India then became the keystone of the British empire, and the focus for rivalry with other European countries.

Extensive rail networks were built across the country and industries developed. As trade expanded, India became a source of great wealth and prosperity for Britain. In 1877, the British Prime Minister, Benjamin Disraeli, persuaded Victoria to take the exotic new title Empress of India and he described India as the "jewel" in her crown.

Lord Curzon, in the middle of this group, was Governor General and Viceroy of India in 1899-1904. Hunting tigers was a popular sport of princes in India, and the British rulers were no exception.

A widow queue

In 1861, the domestic bliss of the royal household was shattered when Prince Albert was diagnosed with typhoid and died, aged only 42. Queen Victoria was inconsolable with grief and went into deep mourning. She spent the next ten years away from the public eye, and wore widow's black for the rest of her life.

The Queen continued to read state papers, but refused to attend official functions, including the opening of parliament. After a while, people began to lose patience with her. Some newspapers complained that she was neglecting her duties and a few people began to suggest that the country might be better off without a monarchy at all.

> "To lose one's partner in life is... like losing half of one's body and soul, torn forcibly away."
>
> Queen Victoria, writing about her grief at Prince Albert's death

In this photograph, taken not long after Albert's death, the grieving Queen is being comforted by her daughter, Princess Helena.

John Brown, in highland dress, takes the mourning Queen out on her horse.

Some people nicknamed Victoria 'Mrs. Brown' in mockery of her friendship with Brown. A few gossips even hinted that the pair had married in secret.

Rest cure

John Brown was a servant in charge of the stables at Balmoral Castle. At the height of Victoria's grief, her doctor suggested that exercise might help, so he encouraged Brown to take the Queen out riding. Victoria formed a close friendship with him, because he reminded her of Albert. But it caused a scandal among some people, who thought that a servant shouldn't be so familiar with the Queen.

In loving memory

Then, in 1871, Victoria's eldest son, Edward, Prince of Wales, fell seriously ill and nearly died. This finally shocked the Queen out of mourning and back to work. But she wasn't going to let anyone forget about Albert. Later that year, she opened the Royal Albert Hall and unveiled the Albert Memorial in London – the biggest and grandest of dozens of statues that she had built around the country in his memory.

Albert's hall

The Royal Albert Hall and the Albert Memorial were built in South Kensington, close to the site of Albert's greatest achievement: the Great Exhibition.

The whole area is something of a tribute to Prince Albert, as it is also the site of the museums and colleges that he set up after the exhibition.

Victorian women

Britain may have been ruled by a woman, but most Victorians believed that a woman's place was in the home, and that the only proper occupations for women were marriage and motherhood. The ideal Victorian woman was expected to be an "angel in the house" – beautiful, modest and virtuous, dutiful to her husband and devoted to her children. She was not supposed to express her own opinions and she certainly wasn't supposed to pursue her own career.

This ideal was reflected in Victorian fashions. Designed to make their hips look wider and their waists smaller, dresses made women look elegant and emphasized their femininity, but they would have been uncomfortable to move around in – and even more difficult to work in.

This Victorian woman needs a team of servants just to help her get dressed.

Women's work

In reality, few women could possibly live up to the Victorian ideal. Most were far too poor to afford the latest fashions and needed to take paid work to support their families. Some were able to combine this with cooking, cleaning and looking after their children, by working at home. They took on jobs including dressmaking, taking in other people's laundry and making things such as match boxes or brushes.

But most women had to find jobs outside the home. The majority were employed either as domestic servants, or in factories where they were usually paid much less than their male counterparts. The hours were long and when they got home they were still expected to do all the household chores.

This woman is a machine operator in a cotton mill. The majority of textile workers were women, but all the factory bosses were men.

Feminine professions

Life could be tough, even for women from wealthy families. Until 1882, a woman's income, and any property she inherited, legally belonged to her husband, even if the marriage broke down. Middle-class women only went out to work if they had no husband or parents to support them. But most careers, other than teaching or childcare, were considered unsuitable for them.

Gradually, in the late 19th century, people's attitudes began to change. In the 1870s, a few universities began to offer degrees to women for the first time, enabling them to qualify for careers such as medicine and law. But professional women were still very much in the minority and they often faced opposition from their families or employers.

Popular politics

British politics had changed little since the 1830s, but by the second half of Victoria's reign, the government began to bring in a number of reforms to improve the health, welfare and education of the population and to give more people a say in the way the country was run.

These changes were partly brought about by reformers within Parliament, but also as a result of pressure from outside organizations. This period was dominated by two charismatic political leaders: the Liberal, William Gladstone, and his Conservative rival, Benjamin Disraeli.

This illustration shows the Matchgirls' Union strike of 1888, when over 1,400 match factory workers protested against dangerous working conditions.

United front

As industry grew, more and more working people joined groups called trade unions. They challenged employers and the government, demanding better pay, shorter hours and safer places to work. When union members wanted to protest about something, they all agreed to stop working and go on strike. Until 1825, it had been illegal to belong to a union, but as the unions grew bigger and more powerful, the government had to take them more seriously.

Casting votes

Gladstone's predecessor, John Russell, had been trying to introduce electoral reforms for years, but the issue split the party and toppled them from power. In a bid to gain popularity for his party, Disraeli pushed the new Conservative government to put through their own reforms. The resulting 1867 Reform Act gave more men the vote and almost doubled the electorate to around 2.5 million. Over the following years, more reforms were introduced, which made elections more democratic and extended the vote to one in three men.

A third way

As more people gained the vote, the old system of government was shaken up. In 1892, a former mining union leader named James Keir Hardie became the first working-class member of Parliament. A year later, he set up the Independent Labour Party to represent the interests of working people. This new third party later developed into the modern Labour Party.

In 1867, a Liberal MP, John Stuart Mill tried to get votes for women included in the Reform Act but he was defeated.

Several women's groups were disappointed that the reforms didn't go far enough, so they stepped up their campaigns for women's suffrage – the right to vote.

In 1897 the suffragettes, as they later became known, joined forces to form a national union.

They fought hard and gained massive support, but it wasn't until 1918 that women finally won the vote.

Hardie caused an uproar when he arrived at Parliament wearing a cloth cap instead of a top hat.

A cholera victim in the blue phase

King cholera

Cholera first appeared in Britain in 1831. There were two further major outbreaks in 1848 and 1854, by which time it had killed around 140,000 people.

The disease struck suddenly, causing dysentery, retching, extreme thirst and pain in the limbs and stomach. If a patient's skin turned blue, it was usually fatal.

This cartoon shows Death as a skeleton, spreading cholera by giving people polluted water.

Health and medicine

Public health improved enormously in the second half of the 19th century. This was mostly due to the pioneering work of Florence Nightingale and others, who made new medical discoveries and convinced the government to take responsibility for the nation's health.

Something in the water

During the 1830s and 40s a number of deadly diseases – including influenza, typhoid, smallpox and cholera – swept through Britain, killing hundreds of thousands of people. The worst hit were the poor, in towns and cities. A civil servant, named Edwin Chadwick, carried out a study for the government to find out why. He argued that the spread of diseases could be prevented by cleaning up the slums.

Most Victorians believed that diseases were caused by foul-smelling air, known as *miasma*, but a doctor named John Snow disagreed. He proved that cholera was carried in water polluted with sewage. In August 1854, an epidemic broke out in central London. By marking all the cases of cholera onto a map, Snow traced the source of the outbreak to a public water pump. When he disabled the pump, the number of new cases of cholera fell instantly.

Waterworks

Gradually, the government took note of the work of men like Chadwick and Snow. It began to build new sewerage systems, improved water supplies and ensured that local councils collected household waste regularly.

Under the knife

Going to a hospital in Victorian times could be a frightening ordeal. Until the 1840s, there were no effective painkillers, and surgeons didn't use anaesthetics to put people to sleep during operations. Some patients were so traumatized by the pain of surgery, that they died of shock. Things improved radically in 1847, when chloroform gas was first introduced as a safe anaesthetic. Queen Victoria herself used it, during the birth of her three youngest children.

Compulsory vaccination for children against smallpox was introduced in 1853. After that, the number of cases dropped dramatically.

On the wards

When Florence Nightingale came back from the Crimean War, she was determined to raise the standards in British hospitals. She set up a nursing college in London and carried out an inspection of British hospitals. She found them so filthy that some patients were catching diseases on the wards, and others were dying from infections spread by doctors who didn't wash their hands or sterilize their instruments. Florence Nightingale campaigned with the government to improve hospital hygiene. Hospitals became even cleaner after 1869, when a doctor named Joseph Lister invented an antiseptic spray to kill the bacteria that spread infections.

This photograph was taken in a ward in the Royal Infirmary in Aberdeen in 1890. It's much cleaner than hospital wards were before Florence Nightingale's reforms.

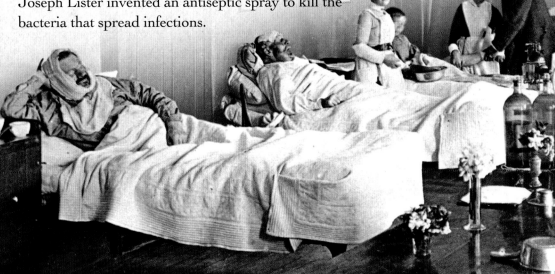

At school

The 19th century saw enormous changes in the way children were educated. At the start of Victoria's reign, around two-thirds of people in Britain were illiterate, meaning that they couldn't read or write. Schooling cost money, which most parents couldn't afford, so many children went without. For the children who did go to school, the sort of education that they received varied greatly.

Boys from wealthy families were mostly sent to elite private schools, where they learned Latin and Greek before going on to universities. Their sisters' schooling was often more limited. They took lessons at home, in subjects such as needlework and music.

For children from poorer families, there were schools run by charities and churches, and 'dame' schools, where unmarried women taught in their own homes. But even these schools charged a small fee, which was often too high for the poorest families.

Victorian children didn't do their work on paper. Instead, they used slates, which were like mini blackboards that could be used again.

Dame schools, like this one, provided only very basic education for the youngest children. They were often more like babysitting services than schools.

Learning to do the laundry (as you can see in this photograph from 1893) was considered a vital part of education for Victorian girls.

Games

Victorians believed that healthy bodies made healthy minds, so all schools set aside a time for exercise.

Most schools had a small yard for drill classes – jogging on the spot, lifting weights and stretching in formation.

Boys at private schools played team sports including soccer, cricket and rugby.

Rugby was reputedly invented during a soccer match at Rugby School in 1823, when a boy named William Webb Ellis caught the ball and ran with it.

Education for all

Over the years, the government began to take more responsibility for children's education. From the 1870s, education was provided for everyone and hundreds of new schools were built. By the end of Victoria's reign, education was compulsory and free for all children up to 12 years old. The nation was now better educated than ever before.

The three Rs

Lessons focused on what the Victorians called the 'three Rs' – Reading, wRiting and aRithmetic. A lot of the work was dull, by today's standards. Pupils repeated what the teacher told them, again and again, until they knew it by heart. Talking in class was strictly forbidden and teachers often beat naughty or less able pupils. In addition to the three Rs and subjects such as history and geography, children were taught practical skills. To prepare them for work in trades, boys learned mathematics, woodwork and technical drawing. Girls were given lessons in cooking, sewing and housework.

Books and the press

Education for all meant that more and more people were reading for pleasure, and demanding cheap forms of reading matter. The invention of steam-powered printing presses enabled publishers to print thousands of copies of books, papers or magazines at a time, and new techniques meant that books could be fully illustrated too.

This is one of Edward Lear's own drawings from his book of nonsense rhymes.

Children's books

In early Victorian times, most people thought that children should only read the Bible, educational books, or stories with a moral to teach them right from wrong. All that changed in 1865, when Lewis Carroll published *Alice's Adventures in Wonderland*. It was written purely for entertainment, and was so popular that it started a whole new trend for children's books. Themes varied from exciting adventure stories set in distant countries, such as Robert Louis Stevenson's *Treasure Island* and Rudyard Kipling's *Jungle Book*, to the nonsense rhymes of Edward Lear.

The Mad Hatter's tea party, from Lewis Carroll's *The Nursery Alice*, illustrated by John Tenniel

Books for the masses

One of the most popular Victorian authors, for young and old readers, was Charles Dickens. Most of his novels were first published in monthly parts, with each part ending on a cliff-hanger, to make sure the readers came back for the next issue. He was also a talented public speaker, who drew huge audiences of eager fans to his public readings, both at home and in America.

The Victorians loved trashy stories just as much as people do today. Cheaply produced paperback booklets, known as 'penny dreadfuls' – including romances, adventures, mysteries and detective stories – were particularly popular. They came in weekly parts that cost just a penny, so almost anyone could afford them. But they were looked down on because the writing wasn't very good and their subjects were often rather sensational.

From the 1850s, the first public libraries were opened in Britain, so that even people who couldn't afford to buy books could borrow them to read. Libraries began to spring up everywhere, and by 1900 there were 295 of them up and down the country.

Writing it out

Until the typewriter was invented in the late 1860s, Victorian authors wrote their work out by hand.

Goose feather quill pen

Ink bottle

Dickens wrote all his books with a quill pen, dipped in ink.

Read all about it!

There had been newspapers in Britain since the late 18th century. But, because paper was taxed, they were so expensive that not everyone could afford to buy them. When the tax was removed in 1855, papers began to circulate more widely and sales soared. A new type of printing press, using rolls of paper instead of sheets, also made printing quicker and cheaper. As a result, many new publications were launched, including illustrated newspapers, women's magazines, sporting journals and theatrical papers.

Newsboys competed to sell their papers to people in the streets.

On the move

By the second half of the 19th century, the Victorians were getting around more than ever before. But in London the streets had become so congested that engineers had to come up with a new solution – going underground. In 1863, the world's first underground railway opened in London. At first, passengers sat in open wagons pulled by steam locomotives. Imagine being covered in soot in the smoky, narrow tunnels!

Outside London, the best way of getting around town was on the buses or trams (buses that run on tracks set into the roads) that were pulled by horses. But, by the 1890s, horse power was beginning to give way to new driving forces, as buses became motorized for the first time and trams switched to electric power. Underground trains went electric too, which made travel below street level much cleaner.

Travel on the underground might have been quicker, but it was certainly dirtier than going by road.

This double-decker horse-drawn bus is covered in advertisements. Passengers on the top deck paid half fares.

Pedal power

Remarkably, bicycles were invented long after the steam train. The 'ordinary bicycle' was the first design to catch on. It was difficult to mount and very unstable because the back wheel was smaller than the front one. In the 1880s, 'safety bicycles' were invented. They were more like modern bikes, with wheels of equal size, gears and brakes. From then on, cycling was all the rage. During the weekends, parks and lanes were filled with eager cyclists, dressed in the latest cycling fashions.

Ordinary bicycles were nicknamed 'penny farthings' because the wheels were rather like two coins: a penny and a farthing.

Need for speed

In around 1885, the earliest cars, known as horseless carriages, appeared. But they were mostly imported from Germany and France, at a price most people could only dream of.

At first, motorists were forced to drive at frustratingly low speeds. This was because a law, known as the Red Flag Act, required all self-powered road vehicles to be driven behind a man walking with a red flag. The law was lifted in 1896, but it wasn't until cars began to be mass-produced in the early 20th century that people enthusiastically took up the idea of travel by car.

The first cyclists often fell off their wobbly bikes.

Safety bicycles had hard wheels, which must have made a bumpy ride.

Motorists were frustrated by the Red Flag Act.

Time out

Until Victorian times, very few people could afford any time out for leisure activities. But by the second half of Victoria's reign, industry was booming and the country was more prosperous. The government introduced new public holidays and limited the number of hours people could be made to work. All this meant that, for the first time, many people had time to spend on having fun.

One of the most popular Victorian pastimes was going to the music halls to see shows like the cabaret announced on this poster.

This cartoon shows a typical Victorian seaside scene. Many Victorians went to the beach fully clothed and rented huts, so they could change into their bathing suits in private.

Day trippers

The trains made it possible for working people to escape the grime of the cities cheaply and quickly, for a revitalizing trip to the seaside. As more and more people flocked to the beaches, Victorian seaside resorts grew rapidly. Hotels, piers, concert halls and shopping arcades sprang up to meet the increasing demand. An entrepreneur, named Thomas Cook, started to run excursions to the sea, with the travel, entertainment and food included in the price. With that, he became the first ever travel agent and his business boomed.

46

Stage shows

Without television or radio to entertain them, many Victorians amused themselves by going to plays or concerts. Bandstands were built in parks for people to listen to string quartets or brass bands. The rich went to operas or classical concerts in plush, elegant playhouses and concert halls. For poorer people, there were music halls, where you could pay a penny to watch comedy shows, acrobats or cabaret acts.

Healthy competition

For hundreds of years, people had been playing many of the sports we play today, but without proper rules. Different versions of the same games were played in different parts of the country. Now people had more time to play sports, and could travel to compete, sports had to become more organized. Players formed organizations to enforce rules and set up local teams and large competitions. For the first time, watching sports became as big a pastime as playing them.

Sporting dates

1863 – Football Association (F.A.) formed

1866 – Amateur Athletic Club established

 1871 – Rugby Football Union set up

1872 – First F.A. Cup competition held

1877 – First international cricket Test Match

1877 – First Wimbledon tennis championship

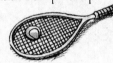

1888 – Lawn Tennis Association established

BROWN'S

THING TIME

Building the nation

Victorian architects and designers believed it was their duty to leave their mark on the country for future generations. And they certainly succeeded. Many of the grandest, most ornate public buildings you can see in Britain today were built during the 19th century.

They may have been building for the future, but Victorian architects were also fascinated by the past. The designs of several buildings were influenced by archaeological discoveries taking place in Europe at the time. Buildings like the British Museum in London were built in a Neo Classical style to look like the temples and arcades of Ancient Greece and Rome.

London's St. Pancras Hotel and
St. Pancras Station (built in
1868-74) were designed by
Sir George Gilbert Scott.

Attention to detail

Victorian houses were often given decorative features. Many of them are still standing today, so it's easy to spot them. These drawings show you some details to look out for.

Roof finial, shaped like a dragon's head, and decorative ridge tiles

Front door with glass panels and an ornate porch

Carved, pointed gables, topped with finials and ridge tiles

Fancy terracotta chimneys

Divine inspiration

But Victorian architects were probably even more inspired by the religion and romance of the Middle Ages. Many Victorian buildings, such as St. Pancras Station and the Houses of Parliament in London, or the town halls in Manchester and Birmingham, were designed to look like medieval cathedrals. This style is known as Victorian Gothic, and you can recognize it by its pointed arches, decorative carvings and high, vaulted ceilings.

When it came to grand designs, the Victorians didn't stop at public buildings. Even very functional buildings, such as factories and sewage stations, were built on a monumental scale, to reflect Britain's great industrial wealth and progress. And many ordinary houses were given some extraordinary features, such as gothic arches, decorative brickwork and even gargoyles.

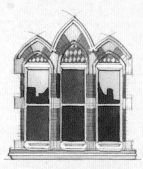

Gothic style arched windows surrounded by patterned brickwork

Engineering landmarks

Some of the greatest Victorian building projects were carried out by engineers. They laid thousands of miles of train tracks, canals and sewers, and constructed huge bridges, changing the face of Britain. Many of these ambitious projects were made possible by the use of new building techniques and materials, such as steel.

Isambard Kingdom Brunel

One of the leading lights of Victorian engineering was Isambard Kingdom Brunel. His first major project was the Clifton Suspension Bridge, which crosses the Avon Gorge at Clifton, providing a vital link to the city of Bristol from the east. While it was being built, Brunel also designed and oversaw the construction of the Great Western Railway line between London and Bristol. This involved building viaducts, a bridge and a 1.5km (2 miles) tunnel through Box Hill.

Brunel worked ceaselessly throughout his prolific career. His many other achievements included docks and iron steamships. Like his friend – and sometimes professional rival – the train engineer Robert Stephenson, he died in 1859 from overwork.

Brunel stands next to the giant landing chain of his steamship, the *Great Eastern*.

This photograph of the Clifton Suspension Bridge was taken shortly after it was completed, in 1864. At 215m (700ft) long, it was the world's longest bridge at that time.

Digging deep

Another impressive feat of Victorian engineering was Joseph Bazalgette's construction of a vast network of sewers under London, which set the standard for cities all over the country. At first, sewers were usually built by a 'cut and cover' method. This involved digging out a deep trench, building a roof and then covering it again. Later, new machinery made it possible to bore far deeper tunnels, without disrupting life up above.

Under and over the sea

In the 1880s, British and French engineers used the latest machines to begin digging a rail tunnel under the English Channel. But the project was abandoned in 1883 because British army generals feared that the French might use the tunnel to invade Britain.

It wasn't just in Britain that British engineers and builders left their mark. They exported their talents all around the world, laying train lines in South America and India and advising on sewerage systems for cities as far apart as Budapest, in Hungary, and Port Louis, in Mauritius.

Building big

The largest structure built during the 19th century was the massive Forth Railway Bridge, in Scotland.

It has a span of 2.5km (1.5 miles) and is still the second longest of its kind today.

The building work took 54,000 tons of steel, 21,000 tons of cement and seven million rivets.

At the peak of the work, 4,600 men were employed to build the bridge and 57 died during its construction.

Victorian art

The Industrial Revolution had a dramatic effect on the British landscape and the way people lived. This gave many artists new subjects and caused others to think again about what art was for and how it should be produced. In the 1830s and 40s, early methods of photography were invented. These provided a new artistic medium and had a huge impact on the way painters worked. Photography also meant that works of art could be easily reproduced, for all to admire, in magazines or as prints to be hung in people's homes.

This is a photographic portrait taken by Julia Margaret Cameron in 1872. The sitter is Alice Liddell, for whom Lewis Carroll wrote *Alice in Wonderland* when she was a young girl.

Pre-Raphaelites

In 1848, a group of artists, including John Everett Millais, Dante Gabriel Rossetti and William Holman Hunt, formed a society called the Pre-Raphaelite Brotherhood. They were influenced by art critic John Ruskin, who felt that industrial life was unspiritual and impersonal. The Pre-Raphaelites believed paintings should convey a moral message – something they thought art had lost since the time of Renaissance artist Raphael. They often took their subjects from the Bible, Shakespeare, and Arthurian legends, painting in fresh tones, with an almost photographic attention to detail.

This is a detail from *Ophelia*, by Millais. It depicts the heroine's death scene from Shakespeare's *Hamlet*.

Arts and crafts

William Morris, another Pre-Raphaelite, was concerned that, in an age of machines, the work of skilled craftsmen was no longer valued. He believed that even useful things should be hand-crafted, beautiful and unique.

In the 1860s, Morris founded the Arts and Crafts movement. He and his followers used traditional crafts and designs inspired by art from the Middle Ages to produce wallpaper, pottery, textiles and furniture as well as paintings. Soon, homes throughout Britain were decorated and furnished in the Arts and Crafts style.

Still lives

One of the first and most influential art photographers was Julia Margaret Cameron, who was given her first camera at the age of 48. She created dramatic compositions by using strong lighting and stage props, and by dressing her models in theatrical costumes. She also took powerful portraits of many leading Victorians from the arts and the sciences. Among her most eminent sitters were the poet Alfred, Lord Tennyson and the astronomer Sir John Herschel.

This is part of William Morris's sketch for Rose wallpaper. He designed the pattern to be repeated over and over, when it was printed onto a roll of wallpaper.

Art for art's sake

By the end of Victoria's reign another new style was emerging. As a reaction against the Victorian taste for moral messages, artists such as James Abbott McNeil Whistler, Aubrey Beardsley and Walter Crane believed that the only purpose of art was to be beautiful. These artists painted in a highly decorative style, influenced by Japanese art, French writers and artists and authors and playwrights such as Oscar Wilde.

"The only excuse for making a useless thing is that one admires it intensely. All art is quite useless."

Oscar Wilde, *The Picture of Dorian Gray*

53

In the home

Housework

Most housework had to be done by hand, so it's hardly surprising that many Victorians hired servants to do it for them.

Carpets were beaten to remove dirt and dust.

Entire days were devoted just to doing the laundry.

Before hanging out the washing, maids squeezed out the water by passing the laundry through a mangle.

Home life improved dramatically for the new middle classes, especially in the late 19th century. Mass-production gave people a greater choice of home furnishings and household goods, and at lower prices. Better transportation also increased the range of foods available in the shops, and new technology allowed gas and water to be piped into people's houses, providing better lighting and sanitation.

Hired help

Most middle-class families employed at least one servant, usually a maid, who visited the house every day to help with the household chores. Richer families might employ several live-in servants, including a butler to answer the door and wait on the family, a cook, footmen to serve food and numerous maids to help cook, serve food, and clean. The hours were long, and there was little time off, but for many people, it was the best way to escape life in the slums.

Mrs. Beeton

Every Victorian housewife tried to run her home efficiently and economically, and there were lots of books on how to do this. One of the most famous was Isabella Beeton's *Book of Household Management*, which gave her readers advice on how to furnish a house, how to save money and what to do in medical emergencies. It also contained over two thousand recipes, and pictures of how different dishes should be served.

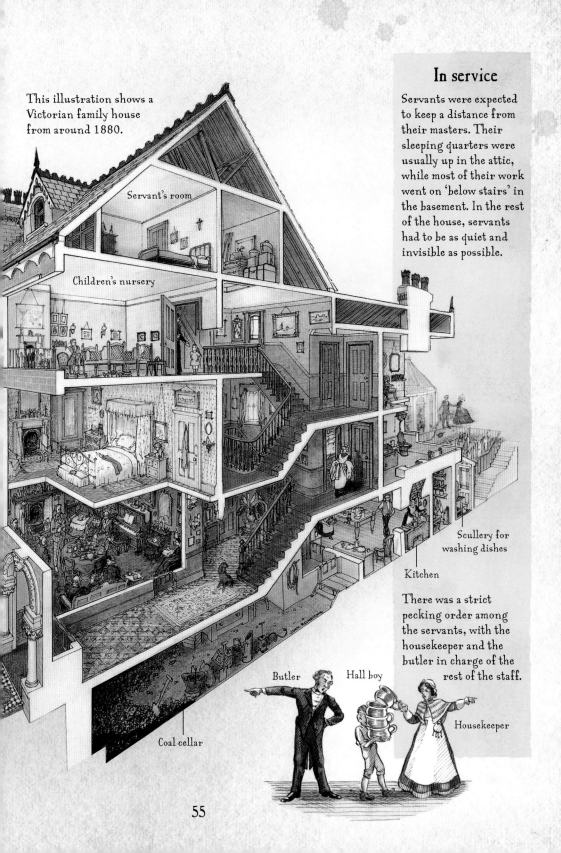

This illustration shows a Victorian family house from around 1880.

Servant's room

Children's nursery

In service

Servants were expected to keep a distance from their masters. Their sleeping quarters were usually up in the attic, while most of their work went on 'below stairs' in the basement. In the rest of the house, servants had to be as quiet and invisible as possible.

Scullery for washing dishes

Kitchen

There was a strict pecking order among the servants, with the housekeeper and the butler in charge of the rest of the staff.

Butler

Hall boy

Housekeeper

Coal cellar

55

Bright sparks

The Victorian age saw an astonishing number of new inventions, which accelerated the rapid pace of change. Some brought modern conveniences to people's lives at home and at work, or helped to improve their health. Others provided new systems of global communication and ways of recording sounds and images, which gave people new art forms and transformed the way they ran businesses, fought wars and broadcast news.

Not all of these inventions were British, but they all had an enormous impact on life in Britain.

1837
The Victorian age begins.

1837
Two British inventors – William Cooke and Charles Wheatstone – invent the first electric telegraph machine.

1837
Isambard Kingdom Brunel launches the first transatlantic steamship.

1839
William Fox Talbot demonstrates to the British Royal Society his method of developing photographs on light sensitive paper.

1847
Chloroform gas introduced as a safe anaesthetic in British hospitals.

1878 & 1879
Joseph Swan in Britain and Thomas Edison in America both independently invent electric lightbulbs, within months of one another.

1877
America's most prolific inventor, Thomas Edison, invents the phonograph, a machine that can record sounds and play them back.

1876
To settle a bet, photographer Eadweard Muybridge takes a series of photographs, each a fraction of a second apart. It's the first step in the development of moving pictures.

1881
Emile Berliner, a German scientist working in America, invents the gramophone, a device which plays sounds recorded onto discs, which can be mass-produced.

1885
German Karl Benz builds the first motor car.

1886
Linotype machines enable the text for newspapers and books to be printed quicker than ever.

1888
George Eastman, in America, produces the Kodak no. 1 camera and develops customers' films.

1895
Guglielmo Marconi, an Italian physicist, invents the wireless, to transmit telegram signals on radio waves.

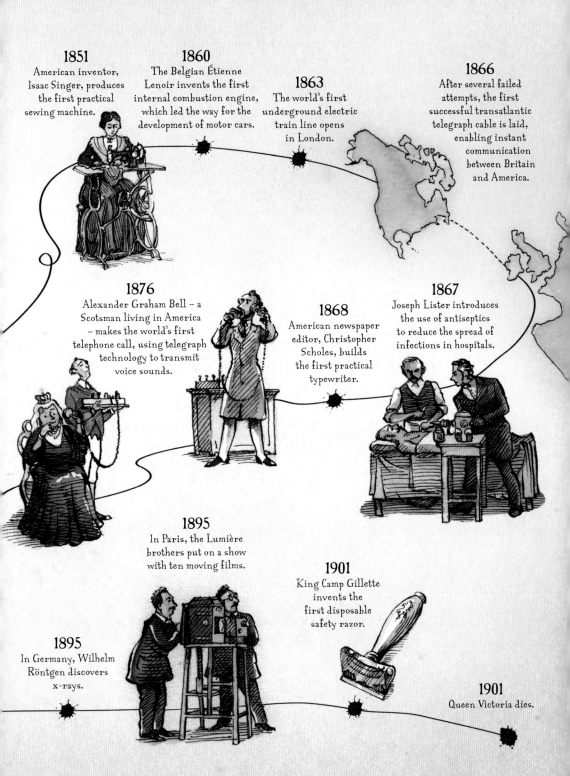

1851
American inventor, Isaac Singer, produces the first practical sewing machine.

1860
The Belgian Étienne Lenoir invents the first internal combustion engine, which led the way for the development of motor cars.

1863
The world's first underground electric train line opens in London.

1866
After several failed attempts, the first successful transatlantic telegraph cable is laid, enabling instant communication between Britain and America.

1876
Alexander Graham Bell – a Scotsman living in America – makes the world's first telephone call, using telegraph technology to transmit voice sounds.

1868
American newspaper editor, Christopher Scholes, builds the first practical typewriter.

1867
Joseph Lister introduces the use of antiseptics to reduce the spread of infections in hospitals.

1895
In Paris, the Lumière brothers put on a show with ten moving films.

1901
King Camp Gillette invents the first disposable safety razor.

1895
In Germany, Wilhelm Röntgen discovers x-rays.

1901
Queen Victoria dies.

One of the first
missionaries in Africa
was David Livingstone.
He explored and mapped
large parts of Africa, and
publicized the horrors of
the African slave trade.

In 1855, he became the
first European to see the
great waterfall on the
Zambezi River. He
named it Victoria Falls.

Livingstone vanished
while he was tracing the
source of the Nile. In
1869, Henry Stanley, an
explorer and journalist,
set out to find him.
Two years later, they
finally met near
Lake Tanganyika.

Livingstone continued
his journey, but a fever
left him in poor health
and he died in 1873.
He was buried in
Westminster Abbey.

This illustration shows
Livingstone and Stanley
on Lake Tanganyika.

The Scramble for Africa

In the late 19th century, the industrialized European
nations began what became known as the 'Scramble for
Africa' as they competed for territory in Africa.
Industries in Europe were expanding and there was a
demand for new sources of raw materials. Many
Europeans saw Africa as the last great unexplored land,
and some Victorians also went there as missionaries,
setting up churches, schools and hospitals.

African resistance

In many parts of Africa, the British established colonies
relatively easily. But against the Zulus of southern
Africa, it appeared they had met their match. Armed
only with spears and shields, the Zulus inflicted a
crushing victory on the better-equipped British soldiers
at the Battle of Isandhlwana in 1879.

The British faced another blow in 1884-85 in Sudan.
A religious leader, known as the Mahdi, led an uprising
against British and Egyptian colonists there. The rebels
killed the British commander, General Gordon, and
held out for four years. Sudan finally came under
Anglo-Egyptian control in 1899.

The British in Africa

The pink areas on this map show African countries under British control by the end of the 19th century.

By 1914 most of the continent was in European hands.

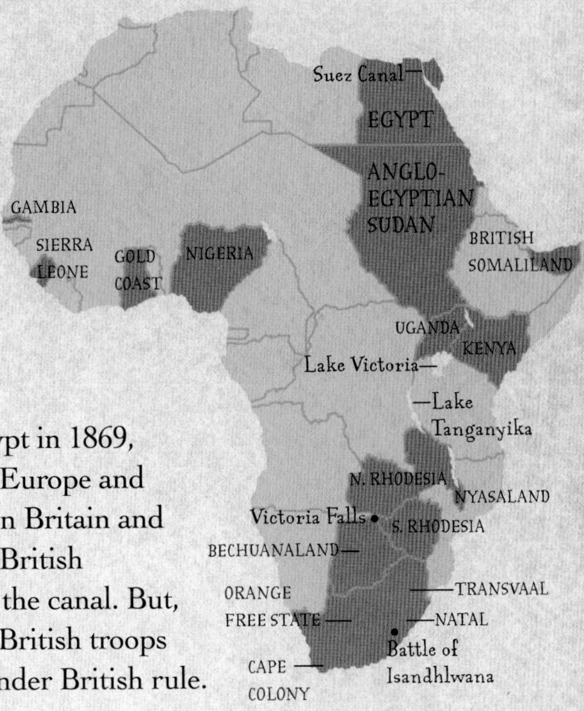

Map labels: Suez Canal, EGYPT, ANGLO-EGYPTIAN SUDAN, BRITISH SOMALILAND, GAMBIA, SIERRA LEONE, GOLD COAST, NIGERIA, UGANDA, KENYA, Lake Victoria, Lake Tanganyika, N. RHODESIA, NYASALAND, Victoria Falls, S. RHODESIA, BECHUANALAND, ORANGE FREE STATE, TRANSVAAL, NATAL, CAPE COLONY, Battle of Isandhlwana

Passage to India

The opening of the Suez Canal, in Egypt in 1869, created a new shipping route between Europe and Asia, which halved the journey between Britain and India. To secure this vital passage, the British government bought majority shares in the canal. But, by 1882, Egypt was close to civil war. British troops occupied the country and brought it under British rule.

The Anglo-Boer Wars

The British and the Boers (Dutch settlers) both held territory in Southern Africa, where fighting over land led to two wars. In 1877, Britain, who already held Cape Colony and Natal, took over Transvaal from the Boers. But the Boers rebelled and won it back after the first war, in 1880-1881.

The discovery of gold in Transvaal led to a second bitter war in 1899-1902. The Boers adopted guerilla tactics, sending small units of men to capture supplies and attack when least expected. In response, the British burned down their farms and imprisoned their families in concentration camps, where thousands died of disease. The Boers were forced to surrender, and their land in the Transvaal and Orange Free State became part of Britain's empire.

The Boy Scout movement was set up in 1908 by Major-General (later Lord) Robert Baden-Powell, a British hero of the Boer War. Today, it is an international youth organization for boys and girls.

End of an era

On New Year's Day, 1900, people weren't sure whether it was the start of a new century, or the end of the old one. But to many, January 22, 1901 was more significant still. That was the day Victoria died and the Victorian era came to an end. Many people looked back over her reign, amazed at the progress that had been made, but they also looked forward to the new century with trepidation.

Despite great progress in health and education, a third of the population still lived in poverty. The country was at war in Africa and the Irish question was unresolved. Britain had led the world into the Industrial Revolution, but now the United States and Germany were beginning to catch up. Britain no longer had the power and influence it had held in 1837.

This brooch was made in 1897, as a memento of Victoria's diamond jubilee.

Crowds gather in London to watch Queen Victoria's funeral procession.

A celebrated life

Queen Victoria's popularity had soared during her last years. Her golden and diamond jubilees marked 50 and 60 years on the throne with street parties all over the country. But her funeral was a more solemn affair. London's streets were packed with mourners from every corner of the empire. Victoria, who had spent her last 40 years in black, ordered a white funeral. Her coffin was decked in white flowers, and it was taken to Windsor to be buried beside her beloved Albert.

In with the new

Victoria's eldest son Edward succeeded her to the throne. He was very different from his mother, who had considered him frivolous and irresponsible. Edward was 59 when he became King. He was popular and energetic, but he had a lot to live up to.

Family album

Queen Victoria died aged 82 – old enough to see three generations of future monarchs.

Her son, Edward VII, was known as "Bertie" to his family.

Her grandson, George V, was king in 1914, when the First World War broke out.

His cousin, Kaiser Wilhelm II of Germany, fought on the other side.

Victoria's great-grandson became Edward VIII in 1936, but stood down later that year so that he could marry an American divorcée named Wallis Simpson.

Index

Acknowledgements

Every effort has been made to trace and acknowledge ownership of copyright. If any rights have been omitted, the publishers offer to rectify this in any future editions following notification. The publishers are grateful to the following individuals and organizations for their permission to reproduce material on the following pages: (t=top, b=bottom, l=left, r=right)

Cover (main image) Private Collection, © The Maas Gallery, London, UK/Bridgeman, **(l)** Private Collection, The Stapleton Collection/Bridgeman, **(b)** Private Collection/Bridgeman; **p1** photo Robert Howlett @ V& A Images/Victoria & Albert Museum; **p2-3** Guildhall Library, City of London/The Bridgeman Art Library/Getty Images; **p6-7** © Historical Picture Archive/ Corbis; **p6 (tl)** Mary Evans; **p7** © Bettman/Corbis; **p8** Mary Evans; **p9 (b)** Mary Evans; **p10-11** © Museum of London /HIP/Topfoto; **p12 (tl)** Mary Evans; **p13 (tr)** Mansell CollectionTime & Life Pictures/Getty Images, **(b)** Mansell CollectionTime & Life Pictures/Getty Images; **p14** © Sean Sexton Collection/Corbis; **p15 (tr)** Mary Evans, **(br)** Mary Evans; **p16 (tl)** Mary Evans; **p16-17** © Hulton Deutsche Collection/Corbis; **p20** Mary Evans; **p21 (t)** © Birmingham Museums and Art Gallery/Bridgeman, **(br)** Mary Evans; **p22-23** Joseph Turner, Rain, Steam, and Speed © The National Gallery, London /Scala, Florence; **p23 (tr)** © NRM Pictorial Collection/ Science & Society Picture Library; **p24 (tl)** V& A Images/Victoria & Albert Museum; **p24-25** © Historical Picture Archive/Corbis; **p27 (br)** © Mary Evans / Iberfoto; **p28 (b)** Courtesy Woodfall Film Productions/RGA; **p29** © Bettman/Corbis; **p30 (t)** V& A Images/ Victoria & Albert Museum; **p31 (b)** © The British Library/HIP/Topfoto; **p32** Ghemar Freres/© Hulton-Deutsch Collection/Corbis; **p33 (t)** © FORBES magazine Collection, New York, USA/ Bridgeman; **p34** © London Stereoscopic Company/Hulton Archive/Getty Images; **p34-35** © Historical Picture Archive/Corbis; **p35** Mary Evans; **p36** Mary Evans; **p38 (tl)** © World History Archive/TopFoto, **(bl)** Mary Evans; **p39 (b)** © Bettman/Corbis; **p40 (tl)** Mary Evans, **(b)** © The Art Archive/Tate Gallery London/Eileen Tweedy; **p41 (t)** Mary Evans; **p42** Mary Evans; **p44 (b)** Mary Evans; **p46 (tl)** Mary Evans; **p46-47 (b)** Mary Evans; **p48** Reproduced by permission of English Heritage.NMR; **p50 (tl)** © Hulton-Deutsch Collection/Corbis; **p50-51 (b)** Reproduced by permission of English Heritage.NMR; **p52 (tl)** © Hulton-Deutsch Collection/Corbis, **(b)** © The Art Archive/Tate Gallery London/Eileen Tweedy; **p53 (r)** Private Collection, The Stapleton Collection/Bridgeman; **p54-55** © John Ronayne/Geffrye Museum; **p58** Mary Evans; **p60 (tl)** © Museum of London; **p60-61** Mary Evans.

Digital design by John Russell. Picture research by Ruth King.